Erika's Story

Erika's Story

Written by Ruth Vander Zee

Illustrated by Roberto Innocenti

Creative Editions ✶ Mankato

To my children. Your stars brighten my life.

R. V. Z.

★

Illustrations copyright 2003 by Roberto Innocenti.

Text copyright 2003 by Ruth Vander Zee.

Published in 2003 by Creative Editions, 123 South Broad

Street, Mankato, MN 56001 USA. Creative Editions is an

imprint of The Creative Company. Designed by Rita Marshall.

Library of Congress Cataloging-in-Publication Data

Vander Zee, Ruth. Erika's Story / by Ruth Vander Zee

Summary: A woman recalls how she was thrown from a train

headed for a Nazi death camp in 1944, raised by someone

who risked her own life to save the baby's, and finally found

some peace through her own family. ISBN 1-56846-176-3.

1. Jewish children in the Holocaust—Juvenile literature. 2.

Holocaust survivors—Juvenile literature. 3. World War, 1939-

1945—Children—Juvenile literature. [1. Holocaust, Jewish

(1939-1945). 2. Holocaust survivors. 3. World War, 1939-

1945—Children—Europe.] I. Title.

D804.34 .V36 2003   940.53'18—dc21   2002073830

First Edition   5   4   3   2   1

Author's Note

✡

In 1995, the fiftieth anniversary of the end of World War II, I met the woman in this story.

My husband and I were sitting on a curb in Rothenburg, Germany, watching a clean-up crew

gather shards of broken roof tile from the city hall. A small tornado had ripped through this

lovely medieval village the night before and scattered rubble everywhere. An elderly mer-

chant standing nearby was telling us that the storm left as much devastation as the last

Allied attack of the war.

When the merchant went back to tending his store, the lady sitting next to us intro-

duced herself as Erika. She asked if we had been traveling. When I told her we had been

Author's Note

✡

studying in Jerusalem for two weeks, she said, with longing in her voice, that she had always

wanted to visit Jerusalem but had never been able to afford the trip.

I noticed she was wearing a Star of David on a gold chain around her neck, so I mentioned that after our stay in Israel, we had driven through Austria and visited the concentration camp in Mauthausen. Erika told me that she had one time gotten as far as the entrance

to Dachau but could not bear to enter.

She then told me her story . . .

From 1933 to 1945, six million of my people were killed. Many were shot. Many were starved.

Many were burned in ovens or gassed in chambers. I was not.

✡

I was born sometime in 1944.

I do not know my birthdate.

I do not know my birth name.

I do not know in what city or country I was born.

I do not know if I had brothers or sisters.

What I do know is that when I was just a few months old, I was saved from the Holocaust.

✡

I often imagine what my family's life was like the last few weeks we spent together. I imagine

my mother and father robbed of everything they owned, forced from their home, and relocat-

ed into a ghetto.

Later, perhaps we were ordered from the ghetto. My parents must have been eager

to leave the barbed-wire fenced section of the city to whIch they had been assigned—to

escape the typhus, overcrowding, filth, and starvation. But did they have any notion of where

they would go next? Were they told that they were being resettled in a better place? A place

where there would be food and work? Had they heard whispered rumors of death camps?

✡

I wonder how they felt when they were herded to the railway station with hundreds of other

Jews. Crammed into a cattle car. Standing room only. Did they panic when they heard the

doors barred shut?

✡

The train must have traveled from one village to another through pastoral landscapes strangely untouched by terror. How many days were we on that train? How many hours did

my parents stand crushed together?

✡

I imagine my mother holding me close to protect me from the stench, the cries, the fear in-

side that packed car. By now she undoubtedly knew she was not headed to a place of safety.

I wonder where she stood. Was she in the middle of the car? Was my father next to her? Did

he tell her to be brave? Did they talk about what to do?

✡

When did they make their decision?

Did my mother say, "Excuse me. Excuse me. Excuse me"? Did she work her way

through all the people to the wooden wall of the car?

While she wrapped me tightly in a warm blanket, did she whisper my name? Did she

cover my face with kisses and tell me that she loved me? Did she cry? Did she pray?

✡

As the train slowed through a village, my mother must have looked up through the opening

near the top of the cattle car. With my father, she must have tried spreading the barbed wire

that covered the hole. My mother must have lifted me over her head and toward the dim day-

light. What happened next is the only thing I know for sure.

✡

My mother threw me from the train.

✡

She threw me from the train onto a little patch of grass just past a railway crossing. People

standing there, waiting for the train to pass, saw me hurled from that cattle car. On her way

to death, my mother threw me to life.

✡

Someone standing nearby picked me up and brought me to a woman who cared for me. She

risked her life for me. She estimated my age and gave me a birthdate. She said my name

would be Erika. She gave me a home. She fed me, clothed me, and sent me to school. She

was good to me.

✡

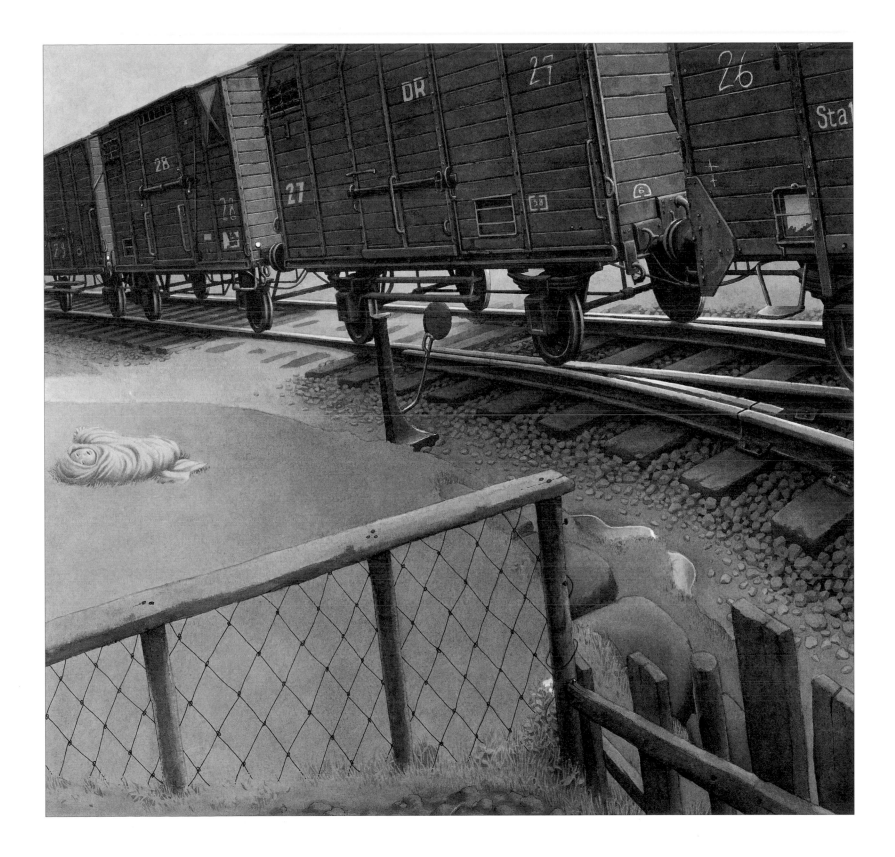

When I was twenty-one, I married a wonderful man. He lifted the sadness that often filled me,

and he understood my desire to belong to a family. We had three children together, and now they

have children of their own. In their faces, I see mine.

✡

It was once said that my people would be as many as the stars in the heavens. Six million of

those stars fell between 1933 and 1945. Every star was one of my people whose life was

savaged and whose family tree was torn apart.

✡

Today, my tree once again has roots.

✡

My star still shines.